The Space Born

MANLY P HALL

The Space-Born: Illustrated Edition
By Manly P. Hall

Originally Published 1930

ISBN: 979-8-90375-011-5
Library of Congress Control Number: 2026937429

This work is in the public domain. The text in this edition has been re-typeset word for word, line for line, from the 1930 first edition source to pre-serve Hall's original cadence, spacing, and poetic architecture. Every poem has been set by hand in faithful continuity with the original presentation.

This deluxe illustrated edition features twenty-nine original works of symbolic art by Charles E. Barbour. Each image corresponds to a poem within the cycle and reflects its transcendental themes through a modern esoteric visual language.

Series: Living Apocrypha
Texts of the inner life that stand beside canon, not beneath it.

For illustration and design inquiries:
Charles E. Barbour — trulytza@gmail.com

For publishing inquiries:
Penemue Media LLC — penemuemedia@gmail.com

Penemue Media LLC
1108 East Main Street Suite 905
Richmond, VA 23219
United States

To the Ascended Masters—Guardians of the Inner Light, companions of the path unseen—whose wisdom, mercy, and quiet providence have guided my steps and strengthened my resolve: I offer this work in reverence and in gratitude.

To Manly P. Hall, whose voice has reached across generations to kindle the lamp of understanding in the hearts of Seekers: thank you for the immeasurable gift of your vision. Your words have shaped my life, steadied my pursuit of truth, and reminded me—again and again—that the soul is never alone in its ascent.

And to Dennis Logan, with heartfelt appreciation for your trust and generosity in allowing me to contribute visually to this masterpiece of poetry: thank you for opening the door for my art to stand beside these pages, and for shepherding this edition with such devotion and care.

With humility and love,
Charles Barbour

EDITORIAL PREFACE

The Space-Born occupies a distinctive place within the corpus of Manly P. Hall. Composed during an early period of his intellectual development, this cycle of twenty-nine poems reveals a mode of expression that differs in method from his later philosophical expositions while remaining continuous in theme and metaphysical concern.

Readers familiar with Hall's lectures and formal writings will recognize enduring preoccupations: consciousness as pilgrimage, spirit embodied within matter, and the cosmos conceived as an interior rather than merely astronomical reality. In this volume, however, these themes are articulated through poetic compression rather than discursive argument. Rhythm, spacing, and symbol carry the weight of reflection. Meaning emerges through recurrence, resonance, and tonal progression.

The poems are arranged as a cycle. Each stands independently, yet their full significance unfolds cumulatively. Motifs echo across the sequence, and the reader encounters a developing symbolic architecture that clarifies through attentive return.

This Illustrated Edition extends that architecture into the visual register. Artist and designer Charles E. Barbour has created twenty-nine original works in sustained dialogue with the text.

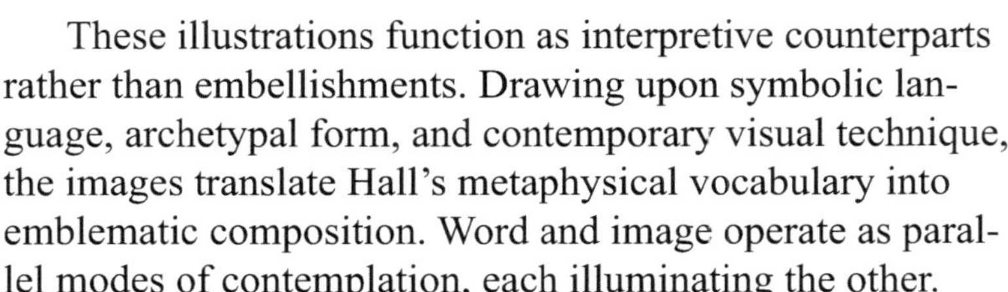

These illustrations function as interpretive counterparts rather than embellishments. Drawing upon symbolic language, archetypal form, and contemporary visual technique, the images translate Hall's metaphysical vocabulary into emblematic composition. Word and image operate as parallel modes of contemplation, each illuminating the other.

For this edition, every poem has been re-typeset by hand from the 1930 source to preserve Hall's original cadence, lineation, and spatial intention. The architecture of the page has been treated as integral to meaning. Hall's poetry depends not solely upon diction, but upon arrangement: pause, proportion, and visual rhythm. These elements have been carefully maintained to ensure continuity with the original presentation.

Within the Living Apocrypha series, The Space-Born stands as a representative text of the interior tradition. The term "apocrypha" is used here in its historical sense to describe works that stand beside canon, preserving symbolic and contemplative insight without institutional claim. "Living" denotes continued vitality. Such texts remain active through engagement, yielding renewed significance across seasons of study.

This volume rewards deliberate reading. Its movement is measured, reflective, and cumulative. Through stillness, attention, and repetition, the poems reveal their structure gradually, inviting sustained encounter rather than rapid consumption.

Dennis Logan
Richmond, Virginia
February, Anno Domini 2026

Not Being *is* my Name.

By

Manly P. Hall

THE SPACE BORN

Due to the high aesthetic standards prevailing in ancient times, particularly among the Greeks and Chinese, special emphasis was laid upon what may be termed the "art of words." Midway between prose and poetry was recognized a rhythm which, though not confined to the laws of verse, left a definite poetic impression. The Macedan Hymns to the Sun, the Oration of the Emperor Julian to the Mother of the Gods, the Moral Precepts of Confucius, the Chaldean Oracles, and even the mutilated versions of the so-called Christian Bible are replete with evidences of a dramatic literary mode which surpasses the grandeur of the Gregorian chants.

Primitive poetry possesses a charm often absent from the more finished products of an age wherein the impulses of the soul have fallen under the dictum of mathematical procedure. During the mythical Golden Age, poetry was considered the language of the Gods, while prose was the language of men. The time must come when humanity again will think, feel, and act by art rather than by rote; for rhythm is simply the application of the principles of harmony and beauty to sequences of words and sounds.

The present collection of fragments is an effort to emulate this style first present in presentation of certain spiritual truths concerning the inner mysteries of life. It will be noted that the various cosmic agencies are personified to render the expression of their several properties more vivid and convincing.

THE AUTHOR.

THE SPACE BORN

Due to the high aesthetic standards prevailing in ancient times, particularly among the Greeks and Chinese, special emphasis was laid upon what may be termed the "art of words." Midway between prose and poetry was recognized a rhythm which, though not confined to the laws of verse, left a definite poetic impression. The Macedan Hymns to the Sun, the Oration of the Emperor Julian to the Mother of the Gods, the Moral Precepts of Confucius, the Chaldean Oracles, and even the mutilated versions of the so-called Christian Bible are replete with evidences of a dramatic literary mode which surpasses the grandeur of the Gregorian chants.

Primitive poetry possesses a charm often absent from the more finished products of an age wherein the impulses of the soul have fallen under the dictum of mathematical procedure. During the mythical Golden Age, poetry was considered the language of the Gods, while prose was the language of men. The time must come when humanity again will think, feel, and act by art rather than by rote; for rhythm is simply the application of the principles of harmony and beauty to sequences of words and sounds.

The present collection of fragments is an effort to emulate this style first present in presentation of certain spiritual truths concerning the inner mysteries of life. It will be noted that the various cosmic agencies are personified to render the expression of their several properties more vivid and convincing.

THE AUTHOR.

Contents

THE
ABSOLUTE

THE ABSOLUTE

I am the Absolute. I am birthless,
    Deathless, eternal;
The baseless Base of Beginnings,
    The Sure Foundation unmeasured,
The Causeless Cause of Causation,
    The Living Root of Illusion.

All these am I, and other things
    Unmentioned;
The sum total of Reality expressed
    In Naught;
Unmoved, unquestioned, undefined:
    I am Omnipotent.

Veiled by the robes of empty space,
    I dream
The troubled nightmare of Creation's Plan,
    To wake
And find Creation's Plan dissolved again
    In Me.

THE SPACE BORN

Worlds are my dreams; the endless
March of suns
Live while I sleep and die
With my awakening,
For life is death and death is life
In Me.

Creation I permit, yet am not of it,
Nor deceived thereby.
Life and death I sanction: they are
Both in Me;
They come and go, yet steadfast I remain,
Unmoved by these.
Wrapped in my seething robes
Of mystery,
Jewel-spangled
By a hundred million suns,-
Lifeless, deathless, being-less, I remain
Permanent, unmoved.

From Me you came, O myriad sparks
Unnumbered;
From my dark wheels I hurled you
Into being.
I gave you selves and robbed you of Myself,
The Selfless All.

Into my embrace I bid you come
Once more,
Fulfilling the law which bids the
Wheels of Being
To launch you home again,
Your labors done.

Of Me you little know, and yet
Am I the sum
Of all that has been, is,
Or yet to come-
The Plan, the Planner and the Planned-for
All in one.

And that One, nameless, being-less,
Hypothetical,
And yet a solid emptiness
That none can crush or bend
Or break, and far less can destroy.
For even destruction
Cannot shatter that power
Which is destruction's base.
No thing by God or Man devised
Can injure Me,
For when all else is fallen, shattered,
Broken-I remain.

THE SPACE BORN

Would you storm my Mystery and
    Seek to find
That which is behind my veil-
    Oblivion?
Then senseless, being-less, creation-less
    Thou must become.

The thundering boom of Silence
    Is my Voice;
Stillness is the herald
    Of my way appointed;
Being-less, I am present most
    When most away.

Not-Being is my Name-
    By no other will I be known.
Limitless, I know no limitation
    Save those passing forms
Which dwell within the aura of my Majesty
    While I permit.

I am the Absolute;
    I, the One before the beginning.
By those whom I discover I am known,
    My secrets fathomed.
The Word unspoken is my Name;
    I am the All-Pervading.

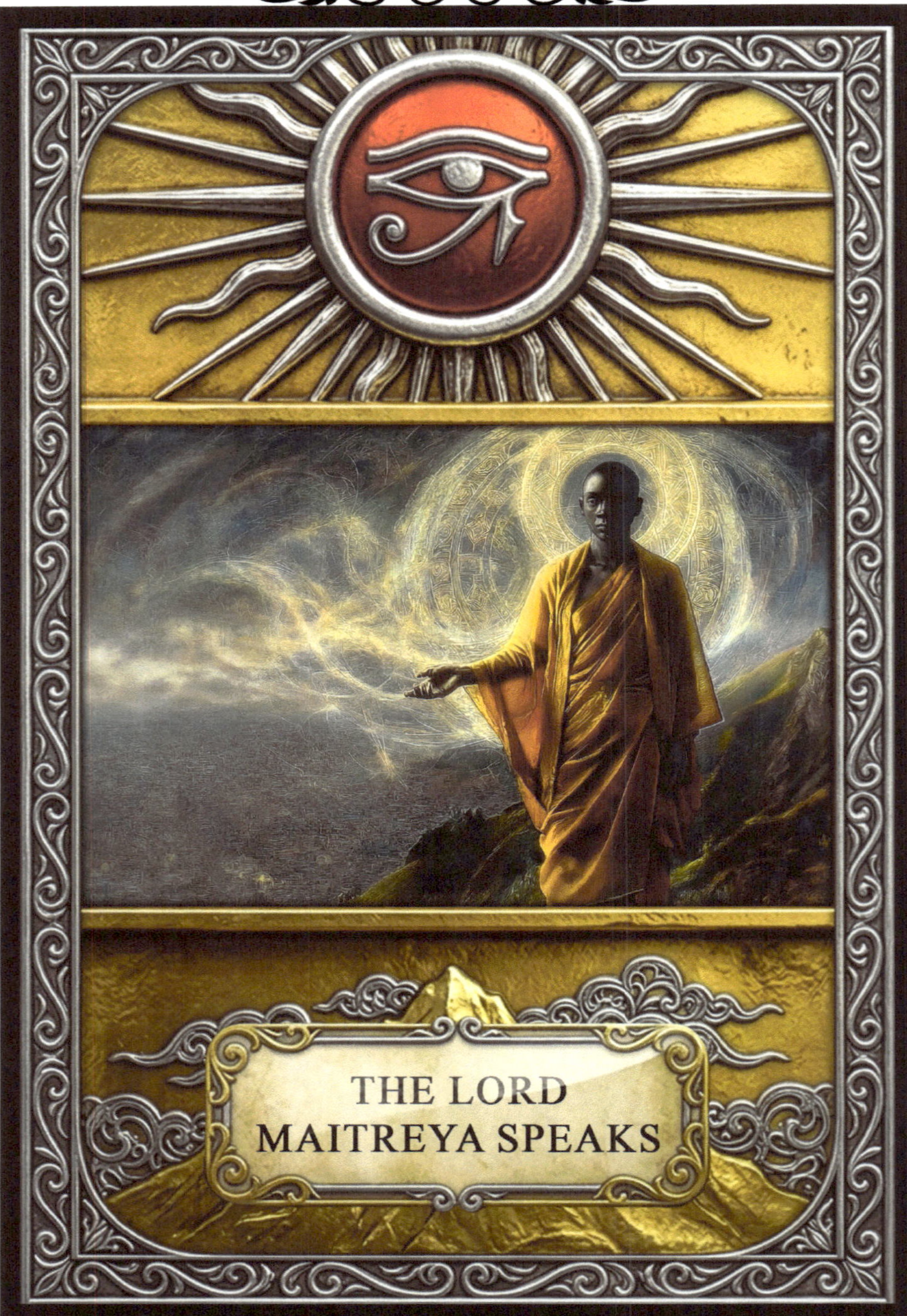
THE LORD
MAITREYA SPEAKS

THE LORD MAITREYA SPEAKS

For all Life's hours of dark
I am the Dawn;
To all the shadowed nights
I am the Morn;
Of all the paths that wind
I am the End;
Through all Life's hopeless fight
I am the Friend.

Who answers ev'ry prayer?
I am the One;
Of all the heav'nly lights
I am the Sun
Of all these circling things
I am the Cause;
Of all this wondrous plan
I am the Laws.

THE SPACE BORN

For all who seek to know
I am the Way;
To those by darkness bound
I am the Day;
For all who struggle on
I am the Goal;
Of all this seething all
I am the Soul.

THE
WITNESS

THE WITNESS

You seek to find among the creatures of the mist One to tell you of that Mystery beyond the clouds, the Mystery that dwells within My splendor.

You ask who has been sent to bear witness of the Absolute.

O blind creation! seek about you. Dwells there anything but that teaches the wisdom of My Mystery?

From that day when time poured forth from Me, they come- the appointed messengers of My way mysterious. To you they bring the tribute of the I.

They serve the Not-self, ministering to the dream in the name of the Reality. The sage, with bowed head, seeks with wisdom to define Me- searching the infinite for word to tell My name or letters with which to scribe the secret of My identity.

The seer, who, with clearer eye,
pierces the mist a little way,
glimpses My glory and falls back
abashed, afraid, uncertain.

Written in language that soul alone
can read, painted with pigments for
which mortal hath no name, sounding a
song that note of man may never capture
upon a written page-

When first the darkness of Space was
rent for the dawning of worlds, and
the darkness of Night brooded over
the face of the Shadow; while the Sons
of the Aeons still slept in the arms
of the Deep,

I woke from the dreamings of Chaos
and, spreading my wings, soared like
some bird of the night o'er the face
of the Wonder, and the face of the Wonder
gazed back- its awareness awakened.

And at last I came to rest in the midst
of the darkness. There in a single
night I build Me a city. The footings
were laid in the substance of the shadows, and
its walls were the fabric of dreams.

I called My City the Center,
and all the rest was outside.

THE
SONG

THE SONG

"Sing to us, O Holy Man,
Of those most noble Truths
Concerning Liberation.

"What means thy Saffron Robe,
And why hast thou departed
Into the Wilderness?

"The Kingdoms of the Earth
With all their treasures
Enticed thee not.

"What didst thou discover
In thy solitudes,
So precious to Thee?"

Then sang the Arhat,
In soft melodious voice,
An ancient chant;

And those who stood about
Understood not the words,
But peace enveloped them.

THE SPACE BORN

"What couch more peaceful,
Than the hermit's bed?
What crown more noble,
Than the shaven head?

"What seat more lofty
Than the lotus throne?
What end more worthy
Than to reap the sown?

"What orb more splendid
Than the beggar's bowl?
What gem more precious
Than the Diamond Soul?"

The wondering crowds departed.
The saint remained alone
By the roadside.

He no longer sang the song;
The song sang him.
Behold, a Mystery!

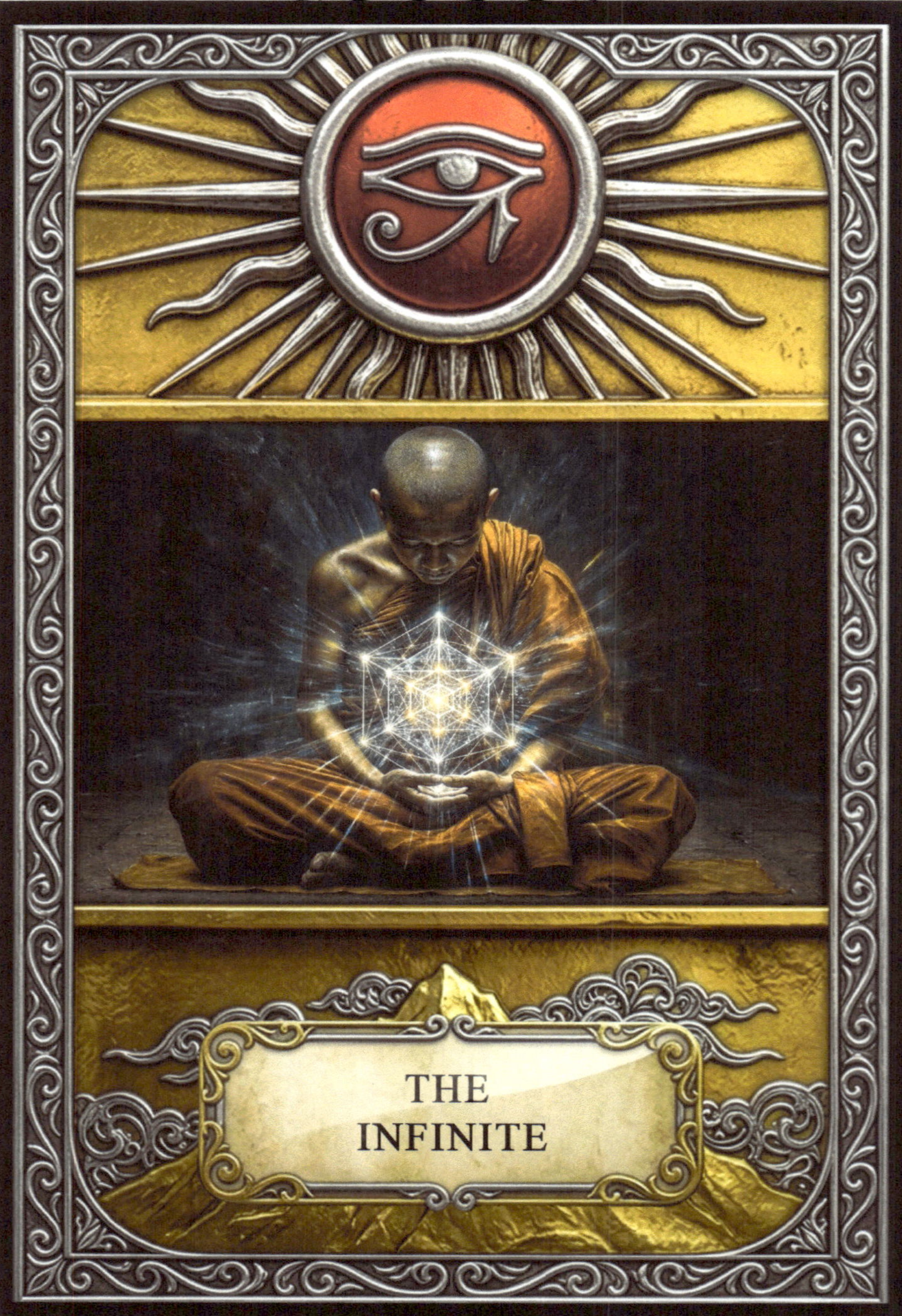
THE
INFINITE

THE INFINITE

Sound is but a shadow thrilling for a
moment through the ether to sink again
into the fond embrace of silence.
Which, then, is greater- the ripple or the
mighty ocean with its many waves and eddies?
Creation existing for a second, then gone
forever, or space limitless, supreme?

Life is the passing of a breath, fitful,
Uncertain; the tossing of a pebble into the
pool- a splash, a ripple, then stillness
unbroken as before.

Time is a dream. Asleep it lies until
Creation forms suns and stars, whose passing
flight gives day and night and murders
Out duration.

I dwell in space. With broadness in my mansion
measured, endless are my domains, boundless
the Spirit that inhabits them. I alone am
free, unfettered, limitless.

THE SPACE BORN

Creation bows a slave to those steel bands of law that are Creation's base. If ye would freedom seek, search not in all this plan. It is with Me. I am Freedom, yet search Me not. For none can share my Liberation till I choose to call form back to formlessness from whence it came.

I am an Emperor ruling only space. I am a Priest giving absolution to myself. I am a Warrior gone forth to fight my shadow-form. I am a Lover, yearning to clasp my bride-Creation- in these arms that close on space alone. I am a Thief, stealing possession that men may value Me the more. I am a Murderer who in selfishness slays all that I may again possess them. I am a Jealous One, fearing for the souls of those that live within the broadness of my presence.

I bow to that ebb and flow that knows no master and serve with perfect sight the plan that exists only when I give it recognition and bid it be.

I answer prayer. I am he who prays.
I curse, and cursed am I. If any strike,
I am the blow and also I receive it.
I am God, Man, Nature, Beast, and Demon-
all in one.

When men barter, I am the thing they buy.
I am the coin with which all debts
are paid. I am the Earth, the Water and
the Air. Flame flickers out my light
and Spirit dwells alone in Me.

The ground you walk upon- I am that earth.
The air you breathe- it is my breath
which giveth life. I am the food
nourishing myself again in you.

Every word my name; every form my body;
every eye seeing for Me; every sense
telling me of myself; every thought
expounding to Me a portion of my mystery
sublime.

I tremble in awe before that Majesty
which is myself and bow before my own
reality. Enter the stillness of thy Heart
and pray for Me, for I, the Infinite, have
need of prayer.

THE
ANCIENT OF DAYS

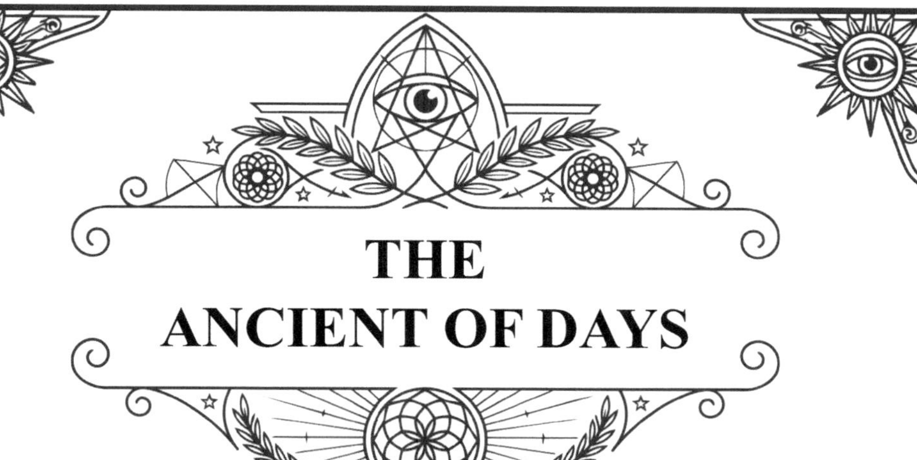

THE ANCIENT OF DAYS

Am I lost that thous shouldst seek me?
In need that thou shouldst offer service?
Speechless that thou shouldst speak for me?

Of height
I am the Pinnacle;
Of depth
The deepness Absolute;
Of width
The wideness Measureless;
Of in
I am, forsooth, the Center;
Of out
The Far Extremity;
Of all dimensions
The Ordaining Power.

THE
SHADOW GODS

SHADOW GODS

Things, things, things- an endless chain of
Things
Strung like beads upon a single gleaming cord,
A thread of deathless life that knows no end-

A golden thread that winds about, around,
Uniting all in common destiny.
Seek ye the thread; the beads are lifeless clay.

The foolish hoard the beads, calling them Life,
Pawning the real to clasp the empty air,
Stealing a gleaming unreality.

Things are but shadows cast upon the deep
By great winged spirits hovering round the light
That, fuel-less, burns forever and a day.

When night descends, the Shadow Gods retire;
Their strange, gaunt forms no longer shade the
Void.
Reality then rules supreme again.

THE SPACE BORN

This is Reality: all things are one;
Diversity a dream, a soul-less lie
Created to torment all it enslaves.

Birth, growth, decay- these things serve time
And bow before their master- suffering;
Life serves Eternity alone, naught else.

Forever is the day of all achieving;
Eternity, the time victorious;
Duration, the end of all beginnings.

Who lives in time is shattered by its blows;
Who measures things is servant to his rule;
Eternal is the soul that dwells in space.

NIRVANA

NIRVANA

O Great Gautama!
Master of the Humble Way,
Anointed of Reality,
Lord of the Deathless Truth,
Tell me of Nirvana's Blessedness,
The dying out
Of the Three Fires of the I,
The waking of the Dreamer.

Then answered the Buddha,
Prince of the Merciful,
As he assumed the mudra
Of the Great Instruciton.
And the words of Wisdom
Which the Lion-faced spake
Dropped like ripe seeds
From the pink lotus of his lips.

"This is the Noble Path
Which leads to true Enlightenment,
By it those of holy purpose
Approach the eternal
And, mingling their little natures
With the Perfect Good,

Achieve to blissful union
With the Ineffable.

Reality is the Only Beloved
Of the ageless, timeless Self;
And Holy Love
Is a mad passion of the part
To finally mingle
Its small nature with the All
And thus attain
The Deathless, Self-less Life.

While man chooses to be himself,
The Law decrees
That he must live, must suffer,
And must die.
But love enlightened
Desires no other end than this:

SELF SHALL CEASE FOREVER
IN THE EMBRACE OF REALITY."

THE
TABERNACLE

THE TABERNACLE

Yeah Thou shalt depart
Into the wilderness of sound
And there build Me a dwelling
Which shall be called
The Tabernacle of the Silent One.

In the midst of the desert
Of many things
It shall be as one,
Indivisible and inseparable,
And its foundation shall be upon
The Rock of the Beginning.

And a stream of water shall arise
From amongst the stones of its foundation
And, dividing several ways,
Make fertile the aridness
Around about it.

And the name of the Waters
Shall be Blessedness;
And they shall pour from the
House of the Lord
Which stands in the midst of the

Desert of Division.

After this manner shall the
House of the Silent One
Be constructed:
Each of the stones and timbers of it
Shall be extracted from the
Foundation which is concealed
Within the silent nature of itself.
And the beams shall be called
The Chants of Silence
And the spans thereof
The Songs of Stillness.

And the Sons of the Serpent shall come
And with them
The Children of the Raven.
The paths of the desert
They shall walk,
Their shadows marching before them.

They shall be robed
In the sand of the desert,
And their garments shall sing
With the voices of angels;
Chanting with many tongues
The Serpents shall come.

At the door of My House
Their soundings shall cease,
And their voices shall be laid
Upon the steps of My temple,

Their garments of song discarded
Before Me.

And each of the Serpents
Shall enter the soul of Himself,
Thus shall he come into the
House of My Presence,
And the Ravens also,
But they by another door.

And as they enter into the Temple
The Temple shall enter into them,
Until even the grains of desert sand
Shall worship
In the holiness of their own silence.

As sound is born
Of stillness
And will return to the source
Of itself,
Of the serpents were born
Of the Tabernacle
But must shed their skins if they
Would enter it again.

My Temple stands
In the midst of the desert of Sounds,
But Stillness
Is supreme
Within the vaulted arches of it.

THE
ROBES OF GLORY

THE ROBES OF GLORY

This I would say concerning the vestments of sanctuary, for my priests shall clothe themselves in Me: My righteousness shall be their protection, for no man bears witness of Me until my splendor has absorbed him into The glory of my radiance.

I dwell in the midst of mine anointed.
They are lamps unto the glory of my oil,
For I am a fuel rising up within them,
Feeding the triple wick of their Divinity.

Unseen, I am the source of all things seen;
Unfelt, unsensed, I am the power of feeling
and sensation.

I absorb mine elect into the effulgency
Of myself, until their form and magnitude
can no longer be distinguished because
of the blazing brightness of my proximity.

THE SPACE BORN

Cast thyself, O son of man, into my
blazing Spirit. From my fire thou wast born.
Return to it again- be joyously consumed
by the flaming soul of thy Creator.

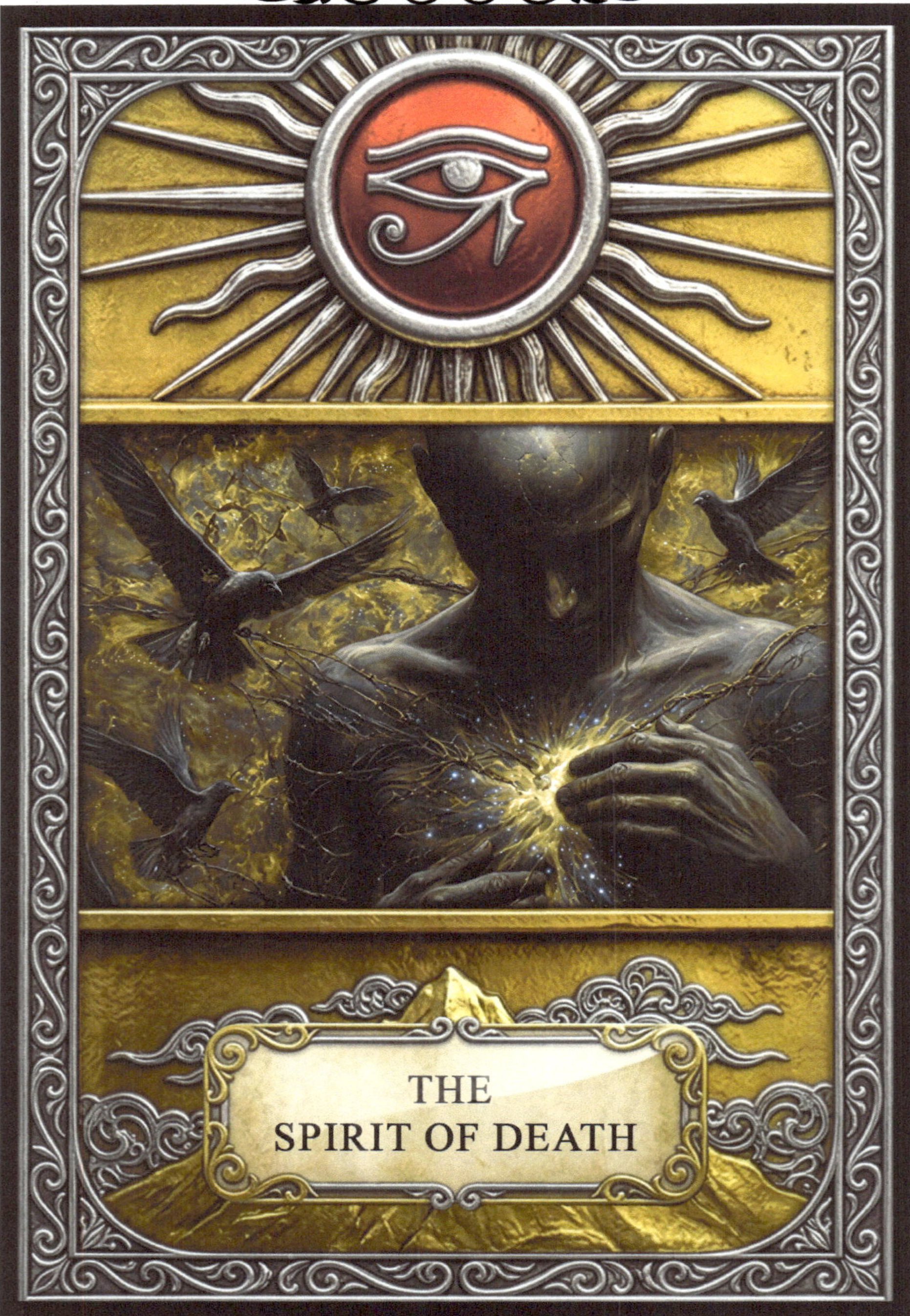
THE
SPIRIT OF DEATH

THE SPIRIT OF DEATH

O thou Spirit of Sweet Release, I name Thee Death and bid Thee serve Me as my messenger, bringing release to those I call from the dark shade that men have named Mortality- the shadow substance-less that all Creation serves in ignorance, bowing before a fond illusion, the fabric of a dream woven from the threads of life and death upon a loom suspended only by the senseless Dreamer.

Thou, O Death, art Lord of all this dream. It dwells in Thee and by thy sanction is. Thou art the entrance in, the gate that leads into the shadow's depth, the path that winds again to Life through that dread door that I am pleased to call Decay.

Faithful One, in Thee I rest the confidence, the trust that unto Thee is power. For none but Thee can bring back to my arms the Creation I adore.

Behind thy mask of ill a Savior stands.
I know for I have made and chosen; and who
Knows better than the maker the thing He
would devise, or who can judge the merits
of the Master's craft or the end which
He desires?

If I be limitless, all-powerful, infinite,
Then in my hands Creation waits the moulding
that I will to give. Then who shall speak if
I am silent, or doubt the wisdom of the way
I have appointed?

Life, Death- I have ordained them both to
the peculiar working of my plan, for lifeless,
Deathless, I alone have power to give
command to anything. Life dwells in Me
cloaked by the veil of Death.

If thou wouldst vanquish Death, tear the
sombre mask away and bow o'erpowered-
for the shining visage thou beholdest is
deathless, terrible in splendor. This is
my appointed Son, whom all men hate until
they have unveiled.

Through the gray clouds of doubt Death
comes to set Life free. It shatters the
clay fetters of limitation, bringing sweet
release. Wide swings the door. I, in my
wisdom, have appointed a place of rest.

Two manner of things hath Death dominion over: the thing unfinished, broken, shattered in the making. I recall it to mould afresh and send forth again to better destiny, a fruitage more complete.

Death also hath the power to call a thing Which hath accomplished from the shadow of its labor done. The ministry of sweet release is in its hands. Discern the wisdom of the One who placed it there.

I blessed Creation most when Death I gave, That Life within the shade might have an end. Through Death alone can men escape the path that, save for Death, is an endless chain of shadowed mockery.

Life hath its ministry. It is a part, an incident in an endless chain of incidents born in the shadow of my Infinite Will to vanish again into the Mystery whence it came, with Death the Keeper of the Riddle.

MIND

MIND

Mortal Mind climbed upward
To the High Place of the Universe.

As it stood alone
Gazing into the Fields of Eternity,
A great fear possessed Mortal Mind.
It cried aloud,
And these were its words:

"Behold, I am alone,
Surrounded by the Great Emptiness
Which is called Space."

And a voice out of Space
Answered thus to Mortal Mind:

"Nay, I am all fullness.
It is you who are an emptiness
Existing for an instant in Me."

EPISTOLARY

EPISTOLARY

Unto the brethren of the seven paths
And they of a kindred spirit,
GREETINGS:

May your just labors be crowned with reward
and your holy aspirations be realized
for the glory of our Lord Jesus Christ.

Concerning those things which are your
responsibilities before men, in the name
of our Lord I would have words with you.

You live in a time of enlightenment on a
number of things, but concerning those which
are of the spirit you are in great darkness.

For, behold! you have blinded the eyes of
your spirits as did the Philistines the
eyes of Samson. You have chained your divine
spirit to the grindstone of materiality with
many bonds and fetters.

THE SPACE BORN

To give wisdom is the pleasure of the Lord.
To sense that wisdom is the duty of honest men.
In this duty you have been negligent;
therefore, are we dissatisfied with you.

For, behold! I have sent out my spirit as a
bird over the surface of the deep, but there
was no dwelling place for it in the darkness
and my spirit returned to me again.

Therefore, will I again send it forth when
it pleases me, that my spirit may at
last find resting place in the abode of shadows.

Why have you not prepared a dwelling for my
spirit that it might rule you in righteousness
and in power?

Why have you not built a mountain for me in
the midst of the darkness and in the midst
of the waters that I might there raise
my tabernacle among my children?

Know you not that One and One alone is good;
that but One is great, but One is pure,
but One is of perfect virtue, but One is
of true discernment, but One is truly
upright- and that One the living God?

Therefore, my brethren, if you would serve the greatest good, abide in the law of the living God, for in that is the path of sure procedure. Be diligent in all your works that they may bear true witness to you before all nations and all worlds.

It is my prayer that upon you shall rest the spirit of our Lord Jesus Christ forever and ever. Amen.

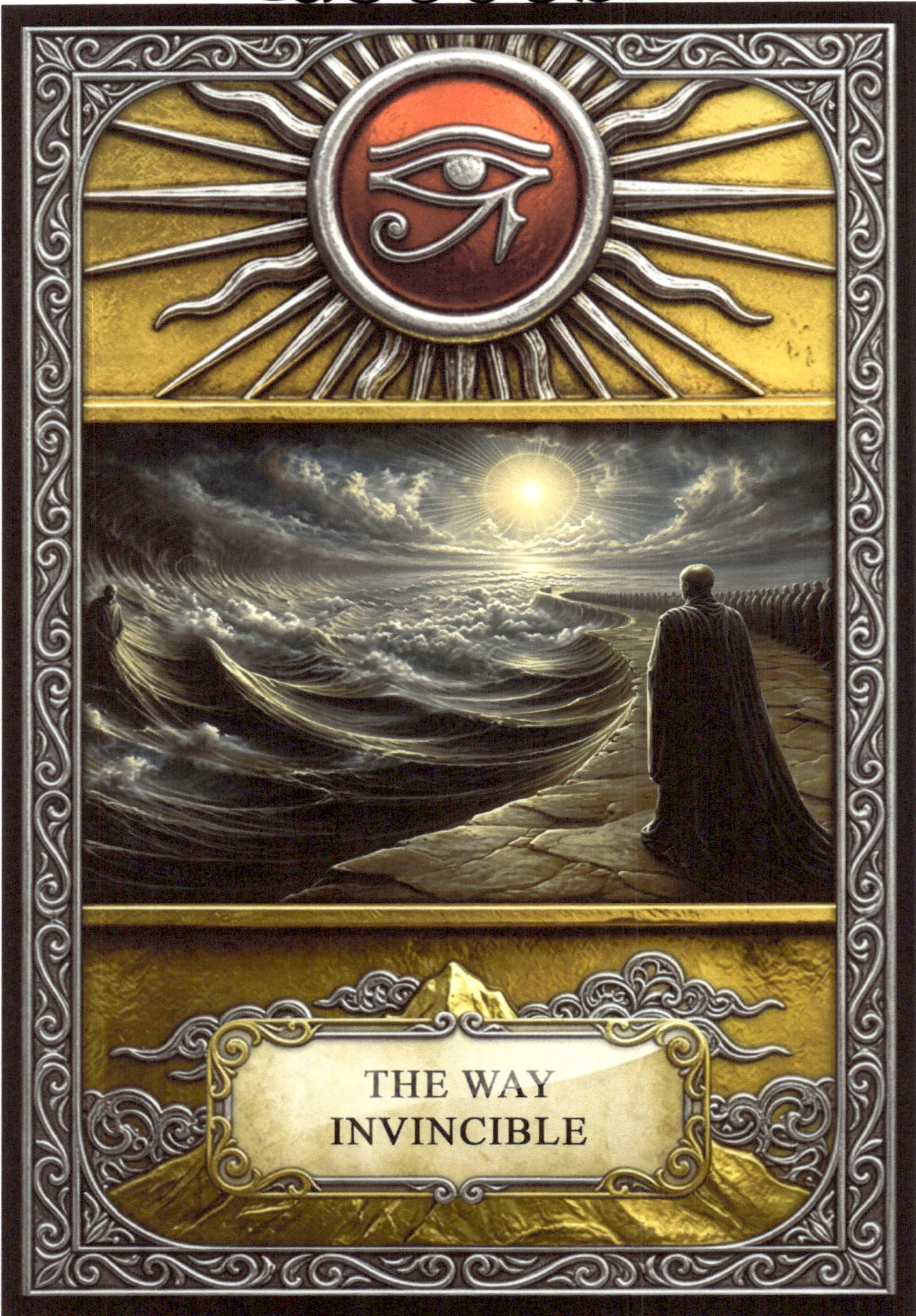
THE WAY
INVINCIBLE

THE WAY INVINCIBLE

Children of the Mist!
Turn back to Me.
Hark to the words of thy creator,
OM:
Truth dwells not in the shade,
Why seek it there?

Truth dwells in Me.
I am Reality.
All else imperfect is.
My virtue is completion.
Creation thunders on the path I have attained.

I am the Lord of All.
Hear now my edict:
Mine is the power and mine the power alone
To weigh, to judge, to measure or condemn

THE SPACE BORN

Who speaks for Me?
Let him stand forth
And trump his triumphs to the seven skies.
For who shall say him nay,
Or who condemn?

Who judges such a one,
Let him stand forth-
Judge, jurors and accused, a seemly group.
What witness can they call
If I be silent?

If I speak not, men mumble idle words.
If I judge not, then justice is withheld.
When I am silent, silence is supreme.
And I
AM SILENT.

Well I know the needs of my creations:
With wisdom I have planned
This thundering scheme,
With strength of hand
Maintain it to the end.

My will must be the cosmic urge,
My word the law that all must follow;
My example, the way of all attainment.
Then mark them well:

Patience in all things,
And in all things love;
Wisdom in all things,
And in all things truth;
Justice in all things,
And in all things law.

These are my ways .
And all of my creations
Are most like gods
When most like gods they act
And learn to wield the power that gods possess.

Silence is the Way Invincible.
None can withstand the force of stillness.
The measure of true greatness
Lies not in wrangling
Nor in many words,
But silence.

Silence is the friend of the philosopher.
The sage is waited on by that deep hush
That brings the gifts of wisdom
To such as can invoke it.

THE
HYMN OF BIRTH

THE HYMN OF BIRTH

A thrilling through the darkness-
A deadly hush-
Space shuddering, Chaos reeling,
Mindless but aware-
Eterenity in the throes of agony immortal:
          Thus Gods are born.

A seething in substance-
An endless twisting-

Groans of swirling ether,
Throbbings in space-writhing sparks
Like tortured souls in Hell's embrace:
          Thus worlds are born.

A cry in the darkness of the night-
A sob-
Shudders that chill the soul,
Fingers twisting, untwisting,
A pale face drawn by mortal pain supreme:
          Thus men are born.

THE SPACE BORN

A broken heart-
A spirit shattered by the blows-
Hands clasped in prayer,
A tear-stained face, an ache within
No human power can heal:
Thus souls are born.

WORDS,
WORDS, WORDS

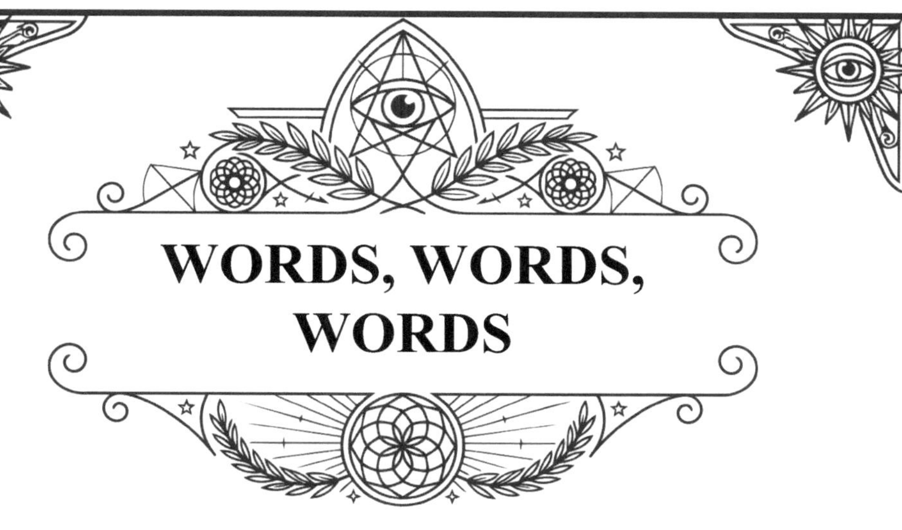

WORDS, WORDS, WORDS

I was lifted into the presence of the Innermost;
I gazed into the depthless eyes of Space;
I questioned the face of the Inscrutable,
And these were the words which I spake:

"Reveal to me, O Thrice Hidden Mystery,
The substance of that fond Illusion
Which men call Hope."

And, as though oppressed with a great weariness,
The Eternal Splendor answered:

> "I dreamed that I was;
> I dreamed that I awoke;
> I was."

A second time I questioned the Inscrutable,
And these were the words which I spake:

"Reveal to me, O Thrice Hidden Mystery,
The Substance of that dread Illusion
Which men call Despair."

And, as though oppressed with a great weariness,
The Eternal Splendor answered:

> "I dreamed that I was not;
> I dreamed that I awoke;
> I was not."

A third time I questioned the Inscrutable,
And these were the words which I spake:

"Reveal to me, O Thrice Hidden Mystery,
The substance of the awful Word
Which men call Truth.

And, as though oppressed with a great weariness,
The Eternal Splendor answered:

> "I dreamed not;
> I awoke not;
> I am not."

And all that had been, vanished away;
And that which had not been,
Alone remained.

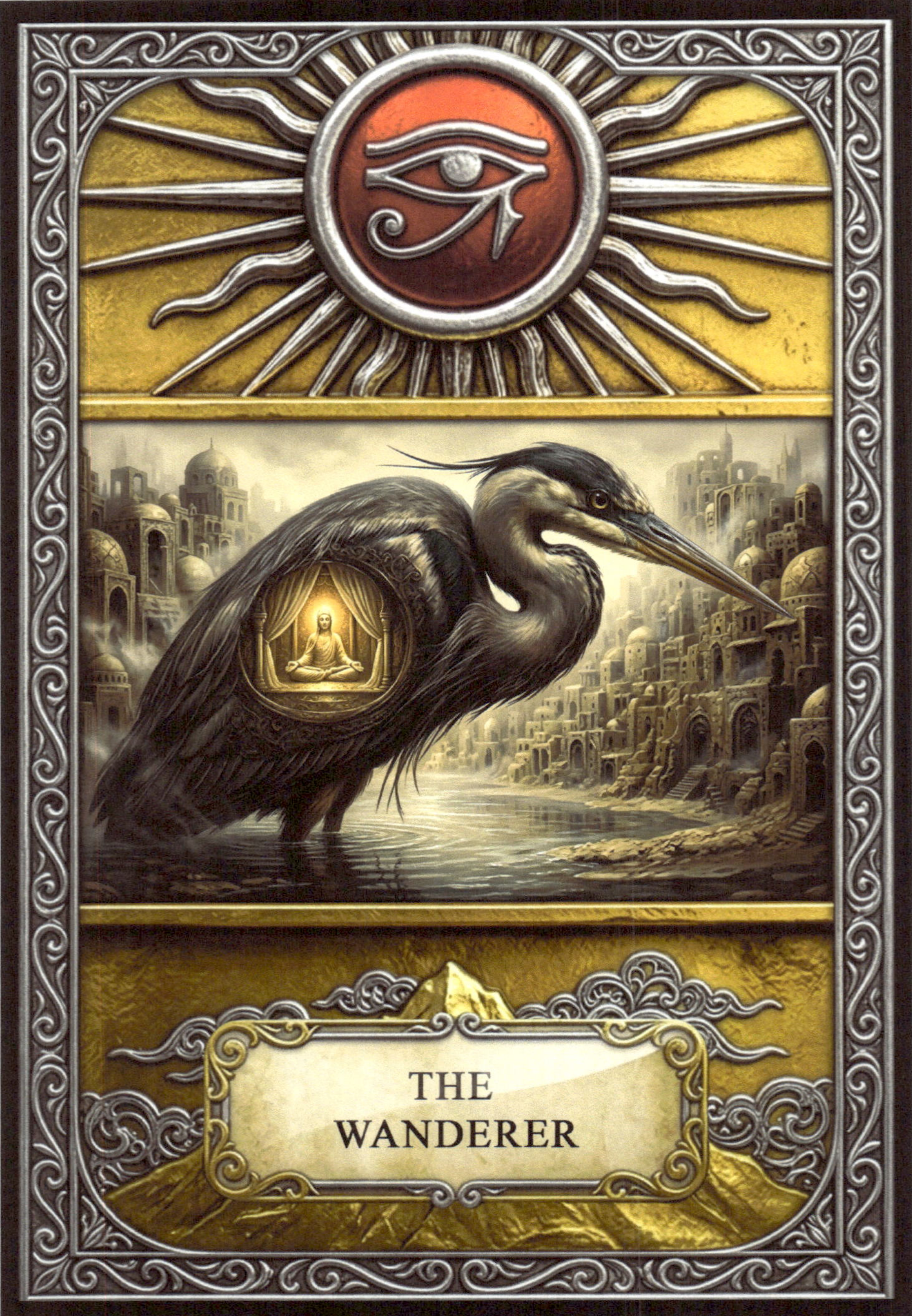
THE
WANDERER

THE WANDERER

I am a Spirit,
A Wanderer come from afar,
A pilgrim born of the Dawn Land-
On a journey unending.
I stop but to rest for a night
In your City of Clay.

I rise with the light of the morning
And continue my way.
The City with Shadows is darkened-
When I leave it behind.
For I am the light and the glory
That shine through the windows.

I am a Builder of Cities
But each is deserted in turn.
I pass from one to another-
Even my rest is in motion.
Behind me the veils of the past, before me
The mist of the future.

I am bred of a nobler race
Than the forms that surround me.
I am a stranger amongst them-

THE SPACE BORN

A light in the darkness.
They cannot know of my longings
Nor taste of my sorrows.

Faint from the dawn of my being
Troop memories dim.
I seem to remember dear hours
When I dwelt in the presence
Of a Glorious One- the sum
Of my Parts and my Members.

I am the Son of a King,
Exiled to wandering afar,
Seeking to find once again
The House of my Father;
Searching through ages unnumbered
For the place of the Dawn Land.

Tonight I dwell in your City,
Tomorrow the City is dust-
For where'er I dwell there is living
And whene'er I depart
There is death.

But I am not dead with the crumbling,
I do not die with the Fall;
I continue my search for the ending
Till I am again with the All.

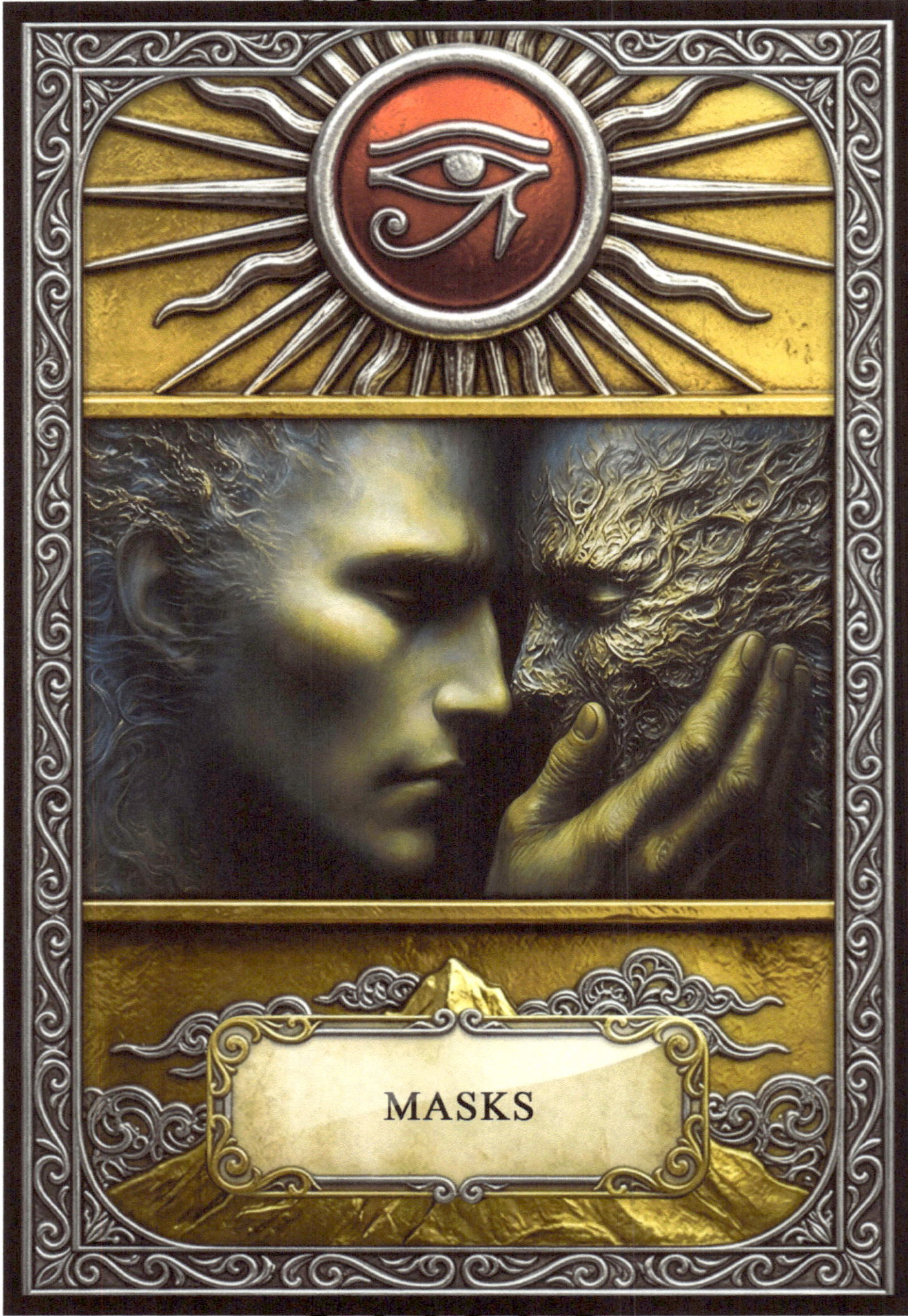
MASKS

MASKS

Some come to laugh; others come to cry.
Some aspire. The most, like cattle,
Follow herdsmen and their barking curs.

Some come to love; others to be loved.
Some come to walk the weary way alone;
While many mingle with an endless throng.

Some come to pray; others to labor.
Some, more fortunate, walk life's way in ease;
While others struggle broken to the grave.

Some come to shatter hearts and souls; others
To have them shattered by the thoughtless ones.
Some come with broken hearts, and others
heart-
Less.

A strange pageantry this thing called Life,
With Death the master of the show, and souls
As thoughtless jesters dancing round about.

Masks, masks, masks – false faces every-
where;
Laughter to hide the tears, smiles the grief,
And flower-strewn drapes the waxen face of
Death.

False faces! See them round about us here.
Doth no reality remain on earth?
Is there no vision through the mask of clay?

Clay, moulded to a thousand forms, remains
But clay, as worthless as before, nor doth
Belief or Unbelief its substance change.

It may be treasured for its beauty or
Rejected because of an ungainly shape;
But loved or hated, it remains but clay.

Our hearts and souls give life to lifelessness,
Tinting the colorless with myriad hues,
Only to find the clay unchanged and dead.

KWANNON

KWANNON

O lady of the sky,
        Thy servant see
And from thy throne on high
        Bend to my plea.

O lady robed in light,
        O Lotus One,
Fair mistress of the night,
        Bride of the sun.

Thou gracious starry maid,
        By Heaven blest,
Pour from thy urn of jade
        Eternal rest.

Incline thy gilded face
        And smile on me,
That I may through thy grace
        Find liberty.

THE SPACE BORN

At thy fair feet so white
I bend in love.
Preserve me in thy right
O One above.

Safe 'neath thy robes of gold,
Against thy breast,
Thou who art ages old,
Give me thy rest.

PRALAYA

PRALAYA

The Light-Born spoke unto the Dark-Born say-
ing:
"This is the mystery of the beginning,
Namely, Eternity gave birth to Time;

"From the spacious dwelling place of Time
Troop incidents, an endless chain of things,
Shadow forms in bondage to duration;

"Suns, moons and stars are incidental;
They rise a moment from the shadowed deep
And, passing through their span, return again

"To shadow; while Time, the heartless Master,
Crushes all, like oxen on the threshing floor
Who with their iron hoofs tread out the grain.

"Unto the winds is cast the useless chaff,
While life with prudence stores away the soul
With true discrimination wisely choosing.

THE SPACE BORN

"Time begot things, and things an endless chain.
Progeny of a dream, well are they named
The great illusion born of difference.

"Back to the unseen worlds from whence I came
To wander but a day 'mid mortal things
I go again, my span of labor done.

"Before me is the swinging veil of mist
That doth divide the shadows from the real,
The veil itself an unreality."

CONSCIOUSNESS

CONSCIOUSNESS

He who shall be called the Seeker
Ascended into the High Place
Of the Mountain of the Wise.

And in the High Place of the Mount
Sat a most Holy Philosopher
Leaning upon a forked stick.

The Seeker addressed the Ancient Sage,
Imploring wisdom from the Master
Who dwelt alone with the stars.

"Tell me, O Lord of the Seven Peaks,
Of the Mystery of Knowing
And of the Substance of Knowledge."

Then spoke the Hoary Saint
In slow and solemn voice, his words
Rich with a mystic meaning.

> "The Knower cannot Know.
> There is no Knowing.
> Knowledge is not."

Bowing his head in helplessness,
The Seeker asked another question:
"Reveal then, O Sage, the inner fact."

He who leaned upon the forked stick,
Smiled gravely and then replied;
"Ponder well these words, O son of man."

"Consciousness redeems; mind slays.
Mind is man seeking for Self;
Consciousness is the Self
Attaining to the realization
Of the man."

The realization of Identity with Self
Is Identity with Self.
And such Identity is Perfection.
There is no other End
Worthy of the Philosopher."

To say more is to take
From that which has been
ALREADY SAID.

THE CITY

THE CITY

And upon a certain evening Jesus departed from Bethany by the winding road to Jerusalem. And the Twelve were with him but remained a little way behind.

It was late when they had come nigh unto the valley and Jesus ascended the Mount of Olives which stood over against Jerusalem, facing Herod's Gate.

And Jesus gazed over the city
and his head was inclined as though a
great sadness possessed his spirit.
Now James, which was the elder, whispered:
"Behold, the Rabbin weeps!"

Simon, surnamed Peter, approached Jesus
and said: "Master, wherefore dost thou
weep?
Reveal to us thy secret sorrow that we
may share thy grief."

Jesus answered him, saying: “Nay, Barjonas, each man’s grief is his own, nor shall another bear it for him.

As my Father hath given me thee from out of the world,
so hath he given unto every man grief according to his lot. Now leave me and depart a little way, that I may be alone with my stillness.”

The disciples, having withdrawn a small distance, beheld Jesus spread forth his arms toward Jerusalem; and they heard him speak in a loud, clear voice and these were his words:

“O city of David! Thou slumbereth and art not afraid. Thy streets are silent, and thy windows are dark. Lo, even the scales of thy barter and exchange hang heavy with emptiness.

“O city of Jerusalem! Thou hast ceased from thy labors for a little while to seek rest in the darkness and kindness in the night. Blessed is he who at the end of the day layeth down from toil.

“Peace be unto thee, O Judah, against that day that hath no night; for each in turn must wake to that everlasting dawn when toil is endless and sleep hath vanished away.

“Long is the day for that man who is himself the very sun; his heart grows weary for the night than can no more come. He who dwelleth ever in the light groweth weary with much day.”

THE
MAID OF THE SEA

THE MAID OF THE SEA

And the Lord Maker of Mysteries
Gazed down
To the depths that His dreamings
Had fashioned;
And, lo! A sea stretched before Him
Impotently rolling.

And the wash of the waves was a
Music ascending,
Filling all space with its
Cadences mournful-
A dirge to the darkness, sung by the
Flow of the waters.

And the Lord of the Mystery
Reached down,
His arms to enfold the Illusion;
And softly
He spoke to the shadows
Asleep in the depths.

"O Child of the Darkness,
Come fourth

From your dwelling of Mist; awake
        From your sleeping
And rise to the feet of My presence,
        Daughter of Mist."

And a cloud of vapor rose from the midst
        Of the waters,
And the Maid of the Sea
        Came forth-
Robed in the flow of the Ocean,
Veiled in its spray.

And the Lord of the Flaming
        Empyrean
Clasped the Daughter of Night
        In His arms;
And the Troubled Waters were stilled
By His fiery embrace.

The Waters were turned into mist
        By the breath of the Father.
And the Heavenly Fire was cooled
        By the sea.
Clouds of vapor arose,
        Absorbing them both.

This mist was the spawn of worlds,
        Of Gods and of Men;
For each has a spirit of fire
        And a body of water.
Flames and vapor conspired
        To produce them.

DESPAIR

DESPAIR

As the shadows of evening
Were gathering,
I sat down in the midst of
My sadness,
And, gathering my mantle of sorrows
About me,
Enveloped myself in the folds of
My affliction.

In wild despair I cursed the heavens
That decreed me
And the black earth which is our
Common mother.
I prayed that oblivion might descend upon
My spirit;
That I might find rest in the state
Of not-knowing.

I cried my misery unto the somber mountains
And the mountain echoes returned to me
My misery.

THE SPACE BORN

The cry of my soul I sent into
The lonely desert,
And the hushes of the desert returned
My cry again.

I cast forth my woe into the
Ocean dismal,
And the sobbing waves returned my
woe
Once more.
Hopless, I flung my soul into
Eternity
And hopelessly eternity returned
My soul to me.

"Is there no rest?" I wailed
To endless space.
Space whispered back again,
"Is there no rest?"
The mountains bowed their crests,
The oceans wept,
And the desert softly moaned,
"Is there no rest?"

THE DAWN

THE DAWN

I am the radiant Son of the Father,
Bearing witness unto the powers of Him
Who is within my visioned presence.

As fire within the flame, that doth bespeak
The hidden power that giveth life:
I am the herald that maketh known my Lord.

I am the morning's glow, Aurora's light
That, battling with the shades of night,
Sends them routed to the dwelling place of
Shadows.

Of the sun I am its far flung locks,
The mane of the Celestial Lion,
Shaggy streams which are the life of things.

I am the lamp, fed by an oil invisible;
I burn with a steady glow of power,
A light unto the feet of my Creator.

I am the morning star which, rising from
The tryst of night, brings unto Creation
The sanction of another day of wandering.

I am the dawn a hundredfold
Of worlds, of days, of dreams, of aspirations;
I am the light of hope, bathing the illusion

In streaming colors that its sordidness
May be hid from eyes not strong enough
To gaze on Mara's leering face and live.

THE
HYMN OF DEATH

THE HYMN OF DEATH

A darkness rising up on every hand,
A peace descending
Upon the place of strife,
A world that fainter grows
With passing days,
While lights upon a distant shore grow bright:
        Men call it Death;
        The Spirit calls it Rest.
Hands that stretch out across the void,
Voices that call,
Phantom forms that beckon,
A door of darkness opening to a gentle knock,
Revealing a place
Of wondrous light beyond:
        Men call it Death;
        The Spirit calls it Hope.

A loosening of fetters,
A breaking down of bars,
An opening of doors,
A soul, long prisoned, free
To mount the golden ladder of the stars
And see the world that lies beyond the prison
  Wall:
          Men call it Death;
          The Spirit calls it Life.

ORDINATION
OF
THE THREE KINGS

ORDINATION OF THE THREE KINGS

Thou Hallowed Trinity
Born of the simple Unity that is,
Appointed to reflect that nameless power-
 The Flame, I AM-
Receive thy Maker's blessing and go forth
To be his champion among those
 Children of the Mist
That cannot know the light their very beings deny.
I, Lord of All Oblivion,
The Fire invisible,
 Am in your hands.

I am Power dimensionless and Majesty
Uncurbed even by Creation.
 Be kind of Me,
 O Chosen of my Heart!
Remember well who sleeps that you may wake
And dies that Life may come to you;
 And through your beings
 Appointed now

Animate each lump of clay you fashion here in Me,
That it may linger for a day and then return to All.
O, Eldest of all Mortals,
Fatherless, motherless, save for Me,
O Finite Son of Infinite,
Beloved One,
In blessing thee I give thee that
Which I do not possess-
The Power of Will.

With this my mystic wand of Cosmic Urge
Set then whirling the senseless atoms
That compose
My robes divine.
And of these strivings thou shalt build
A world that lives through striving, and
With dawn of peace
Returns again
To those dark shadows of Myself,
Ceasing to be within the dark embrace of Chaos.
Unto you,
Second Beloved of Me,
My Radiant One
Who warms my coldness with the glow of Love,
I give
The triple crown of Wisdom with its seven jewels-
Gems from whose stone souls shines some of
that
Endless light

That even Clay cannot entirely hide within its
Crumbling self, but still bears witness
To my Flame.

Prince of the Bleeding Heart,
Embrace thy Father,
Who, save for thee, would never know
That inner sense that guides the godless, till
Through thy love
I claim them to Myself.
Nor art thou least of Me,
O Spirit of Sweet Deatchment,
Lord Breaker of Things,
Ordained of Me,
Beloved Son.

I bid you serve my cause through fond decay,
And bring at last all things again into
My yearning Self
That waits to welcome, when the striving
Of the sparks is over for a day, and
Fiery dawn gives place
To gentle even.

Of all my chosen
Thou art not the least;
Of all my three, you serve most faithfully;
Thy ruthless shatterings but bring
Reality the closer.

Ye three are the fashionings of my troubled
  Dream
And while I sleep unrealized and unknown
Represented in Creation only as Creation's All,
          I give my power to you,
          Be gentle of Me.

I ordain you Builders of my fond illusion,
Teaching all space to know that
          I alone exist
By proving one by one all other things
          Are false,
          And I alone am Real.

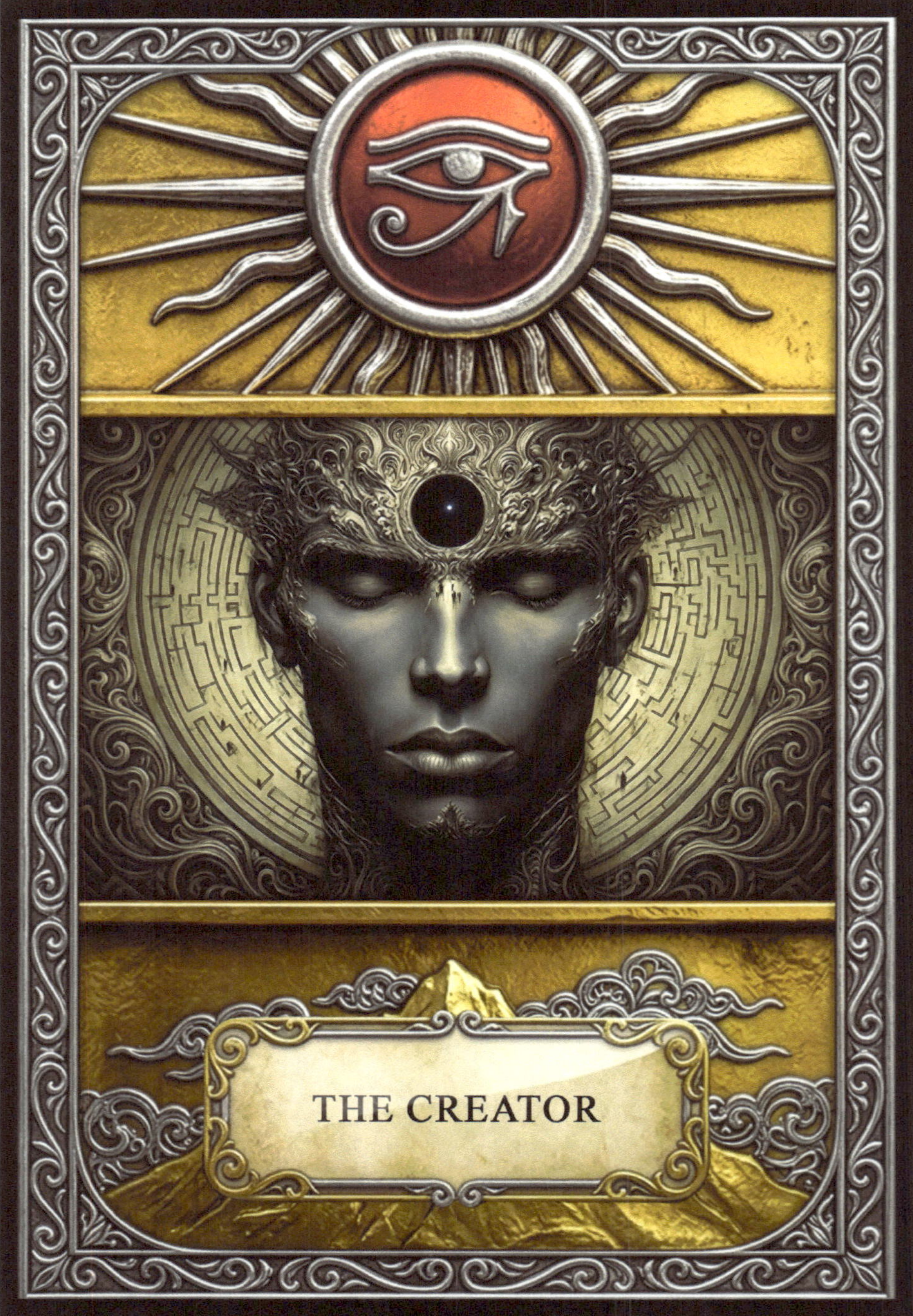
THE CREATOR

THE CREATOR

First the Self-born Lord in contemplation
Entered the state of Unreality, dwelling
For a moment in Illusion. As spirit
To the body comes at birth and dons the
Veil of non-tranquility, so the Self
Within the not-self was immersed.

The Uncreated in His dream became Creator,
The opposites His progeny. The One assumed
The Two, the Two the Three-and thus
The multitudes were born of Him who is
The Only One, and He alone is real in fact,
Permanent and unmoved.

Men live within the dreams of Infinite,
Dwelling in the shadows of His sleepings-
Timeless, measureless, hopeless as a dream.

The Lord dwelleth in His meditations:
All thoughts His thoughts, all dreams
His dreaming-through the Not-self He knows
Himself again.

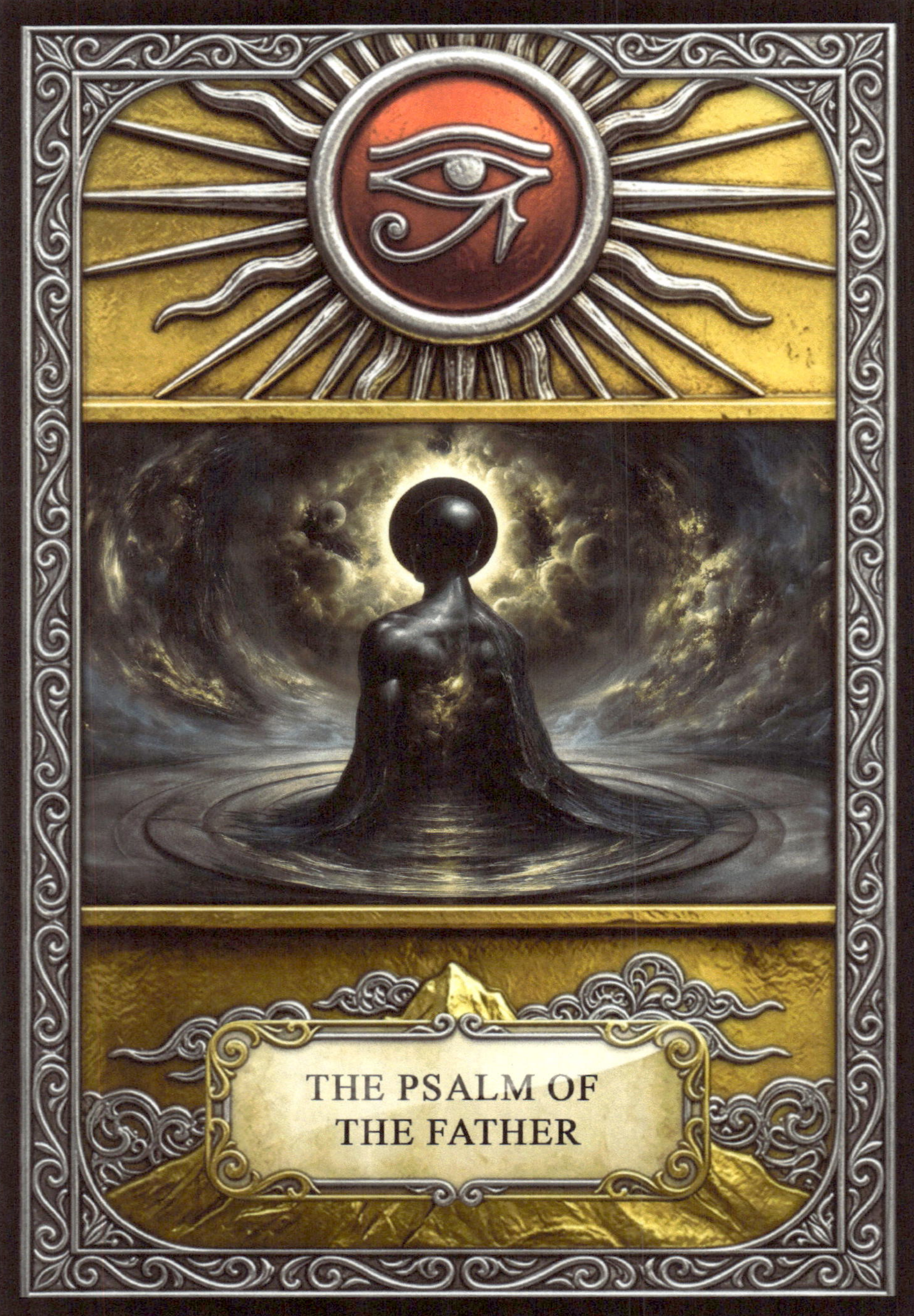
THE PSALM OF
THE FATHER

THE PSALM OF THE FATHER

From darkness unto darkness is my span;
I am the Father of the Darkened Face.
Serene the sea of shadow, tideless, save

For the measured pulsing of my heart.
In all, of all, over all I brood, and see
My shadow mirrored in the formless deep.

The placid darkness changes to a seething
Mass that ever brighter grows with friction's
Flame, a carnival of maddened lights.

I am the Father of the Shining Face,
Flame-born from out the darkness of Myself,
Slaying the parent that the child may leave.

Flames, reaching out to torture silence
With their lurid tongues, meet seething
space
And mighty vapors rise enfolding all.

THE SPACE BORN

I am the Mother, vapor robed and veiled,
Clasping in my arms of vibrant space the
Flaming man-child, born of my virgin Self.

One by one my veils are torn aside, until
I stand in all the majesty of Suns
And Moons that dot the firmament of I.

I am the father of the Hidden Face,
Known to man only as that mystic urge
Moving all things to their appointed end-

More From Penemue Media

Contemporary Wortzs of the Inner Tradition

The poems collected in the space-born speak of humanity as a being poised between the infinite and the familiar, shaped by unseen forces yet responsible for its own awakening.
Readers who recognize this tension as a living reality may find further reflection in the following works, which continue the inquiry in a modern voice while remaining faithful to the perennial concerns of conscience, desire, and self-knowledge.

Available in Print and Unabridged Audio

Many works in this catalog are also available as complete, unabridged audio recordings, produced with attention to cadence, clarity, and fidelity to the original text. these recordings are intended for contemplative listening, study, and repeated return.

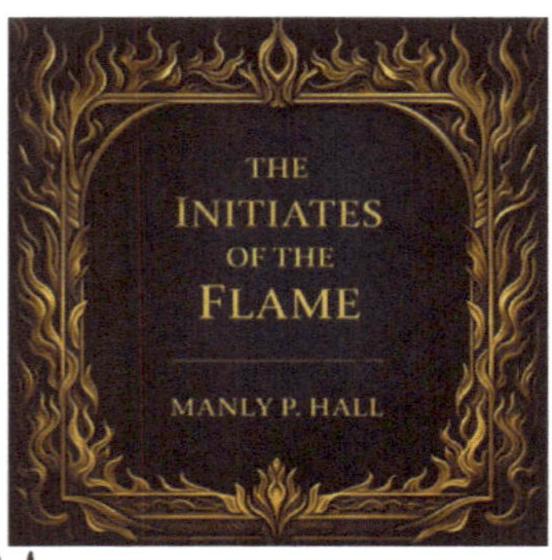

The Initiates of the Flame

A symbolic examinatio of spiritual transformation through trial, sacrifice, and illumination.
This work approaches initiation as an interior process rather than a ceremonial event.

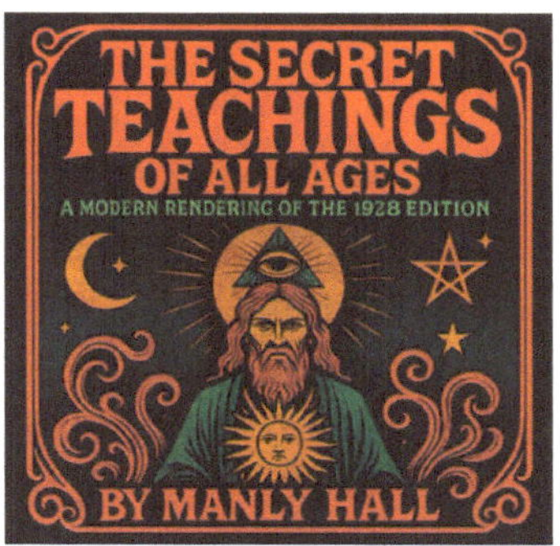

The Secret Teachings of All Ages

A comprehensive survey of symbolic philosophy, myth, and esoteric tradition. This modern rendering preserves the scope and ambition of the original 1928 edition.

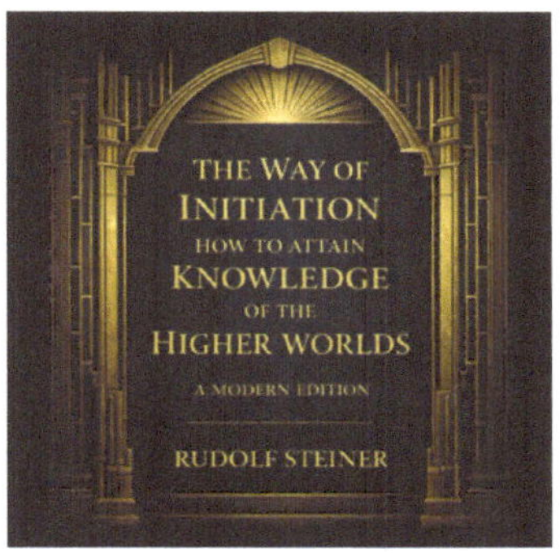

The Way of Initiation

A modern guide to spiritual initiation, outlining the disciplined inner stages required for higher knowledge—faithful to the original method's rigor.

Science of Breath

Complete manual outlining breathing practices for physical, mental, and spiritual regulation. Breath is presented as a bridge between body and consciousness.

The Book of Living Proverbs

A modern collection of aphorisms in the spirit of ancient wisdom literature—offered as mirrors for slow reading and return, not commandments.

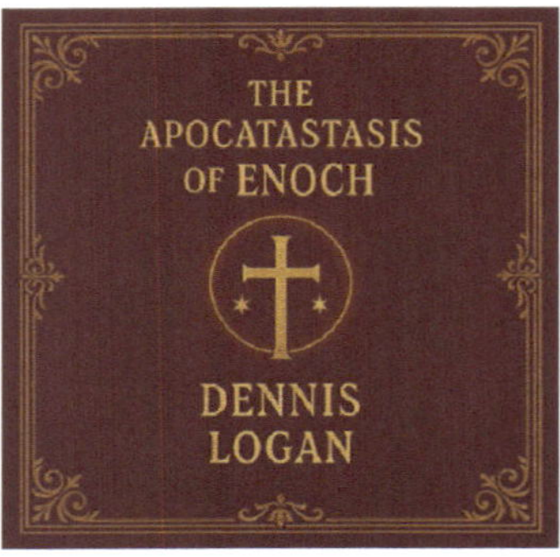

The Apocatastasis of Enoch

A modern apocryphal cycle in scriptural voice, satirical in the spirit of lucian, using prophetic and symbolic forms to confront conscience, will, and the return of all things to their source.

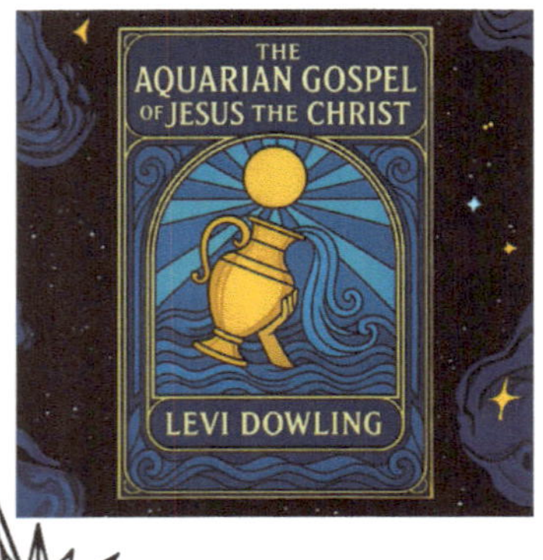

The Aquarian Gospel of Jesus Christ

A narrative account of the life of Jesus emphasizing universality and spiritual development. This text blends scripture, philosophy, and imaginative reconstruction.

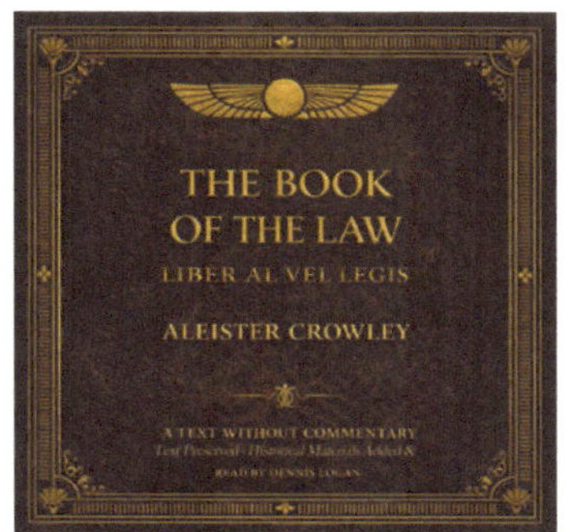

The Book of The Law

A foundational modern occult text in prophetic voice, I challenging authority, obedience, and identity through paradox and declaration.

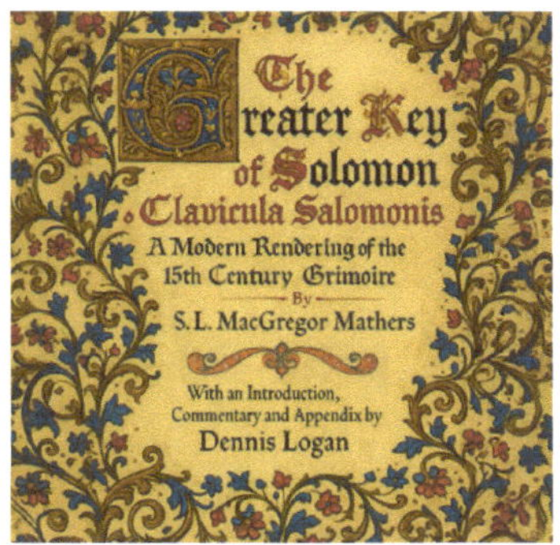

The Greater Key of Solomon

A classical grimoire concerned with authority, order, and ritual discipline. Presented here with attention to structure and symbolism rather than sensationalism.

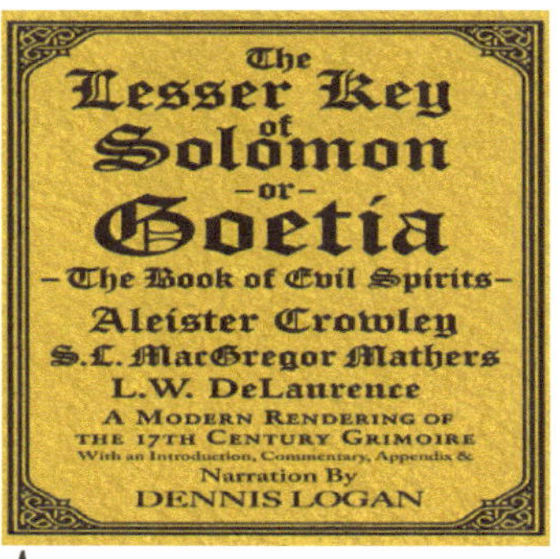

The Lesser Key of Solomon

A classical grimoire of spiritual intelligences and the laws that govern them framed as symbolic order and moral discipline rather than spectacle.

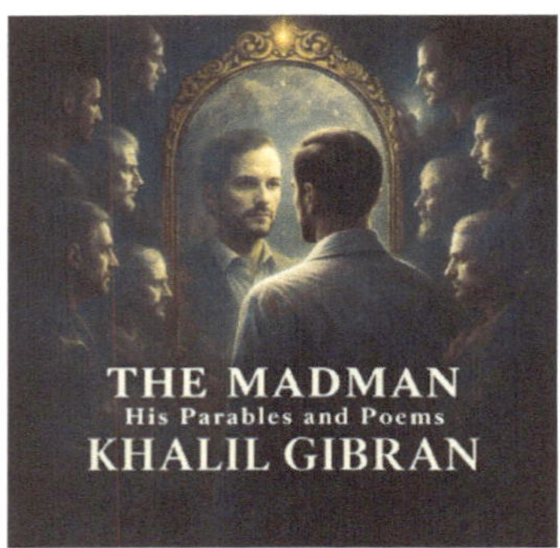

The Madman

Symbolic parables and poetic fragments from the edge of reason, where wisdom arrives through inversion, irony, and the outsider's unsettling clarity.

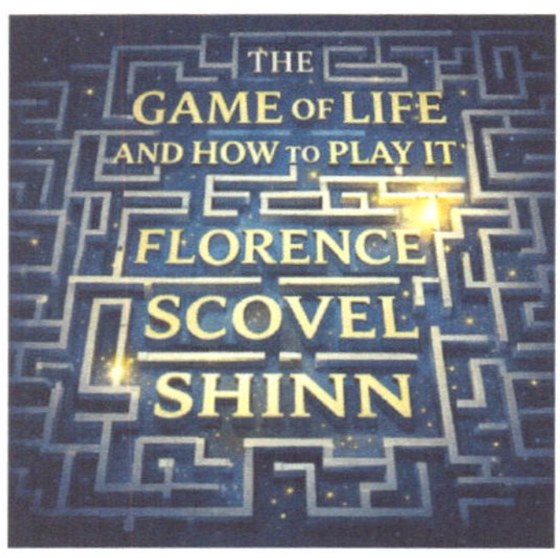

The Game of Life

A concise work of metaphysical instruction presenting life as a field governed by mental law. Its tone is direct and practical, emphasizing responsibility for thought, speech, and expectation.

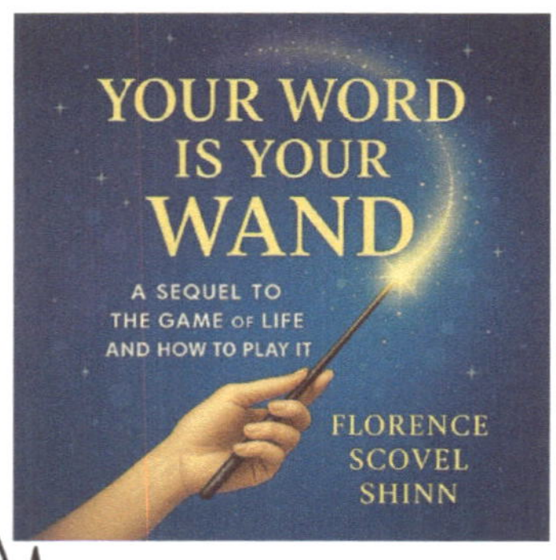

Your Word is Your Wand

A sequel work emphasizing speech as an active instrument of intention.
This text frames language as both ethical responsibility and creative force.

www.ingramcontent.com/pod-product-compliance
Lightning Source LLC
LaVergne TN
LVHW052304100826
845147LV00006B/673

* 9 7 9 8 9 0 3 7 5 0 1 1 5 *